Tons of Trucks!

BIG RIGS

By Martin Harasymiw

Gareth Stevens
PUBLISHING

Please visit our website, www.garethstevens.com. For a free color catalog of all our high-quality books, call toll free 1-800-542-2595 or fax 1-877-542-2596.

Library of Congress Cataloging-in-Publication Data
Names: Harasymiw, Martin, 1978- author.
Title: Big rigs / Martin Harasymiw.
Description: New York : Gareth Stevens Publishing, 2022. | Series: Tons of trucks! | Includes index. | Audience: Grades K-1
Identifiers: LCCN 2020024446 (print) | LCCN 2020024447 (ebook) | ISBN 9781538262719 (library binding) | ISBN 9781538262702 (set) | ISBN 9781538262696 (paperback) | ISBN 9781538262726 (ebook)
Subjects: LCSH: Tractor trailer combinations–Juvenile literature. | Truck–Juvenile literature.
Classification: LCC TL230.15 .H3678 2022 (print) | LCC TL230.15 (ebook) | DDC 629.224–dc23
LC record available at https://lccn.loc.gov/2020024446
LC ebook record available at https://lccn.loc.gov/2020024447

First Edition

Published in 2022 by
Gareth Stevens Publishing
111 East 14th Street, Suite 349
New York, NY 10003

Editor: Therese Shea
Designer: Deanna Paternostro

Photo credits: Cover, pp. 1, 9, 24 (left) Vitpho/Shutterstock.com; p. 5 Bluberries/iStock/Getty Images Plus/Getty Images; p. 7 oksana.perkins/Shutterstock.com; pp. 11, 24 (right) Julie DeGuia/Shutterstock.com; p. 13 Everett Media/Shutterstock.com; p. 15 TonyV3112/Shutterstock.com; p. 17 Photoagriculture/Shutterstock.com; p. 19 smereka/Shutterstock.com; p. 21 Mikbiz/Shutterstock.com; p. 23 rCarner/Shutterstock.com.

Printed in the United States of America

CPSIA compliance information: Batch #CSGS22: For further information contact Gareth Stevens, New York, New York at 1-800-542-2595.

Contents

This is my toy truck.
It's a big rig!

This is a real big rig.
It has two parts.

5319

The front is the tractor.

The back is the trailer.

There are many kinds.
They have special names.

This reefer holds cold food.

123 refrigerated
FAW

This tanker holds milk.

This hopper carries corn.

VOLVO
420
FH12
AT 9334 BK

Car carriers
are big rigs too.

Big rigs help!

Words to Know

tractor

trailer

Index